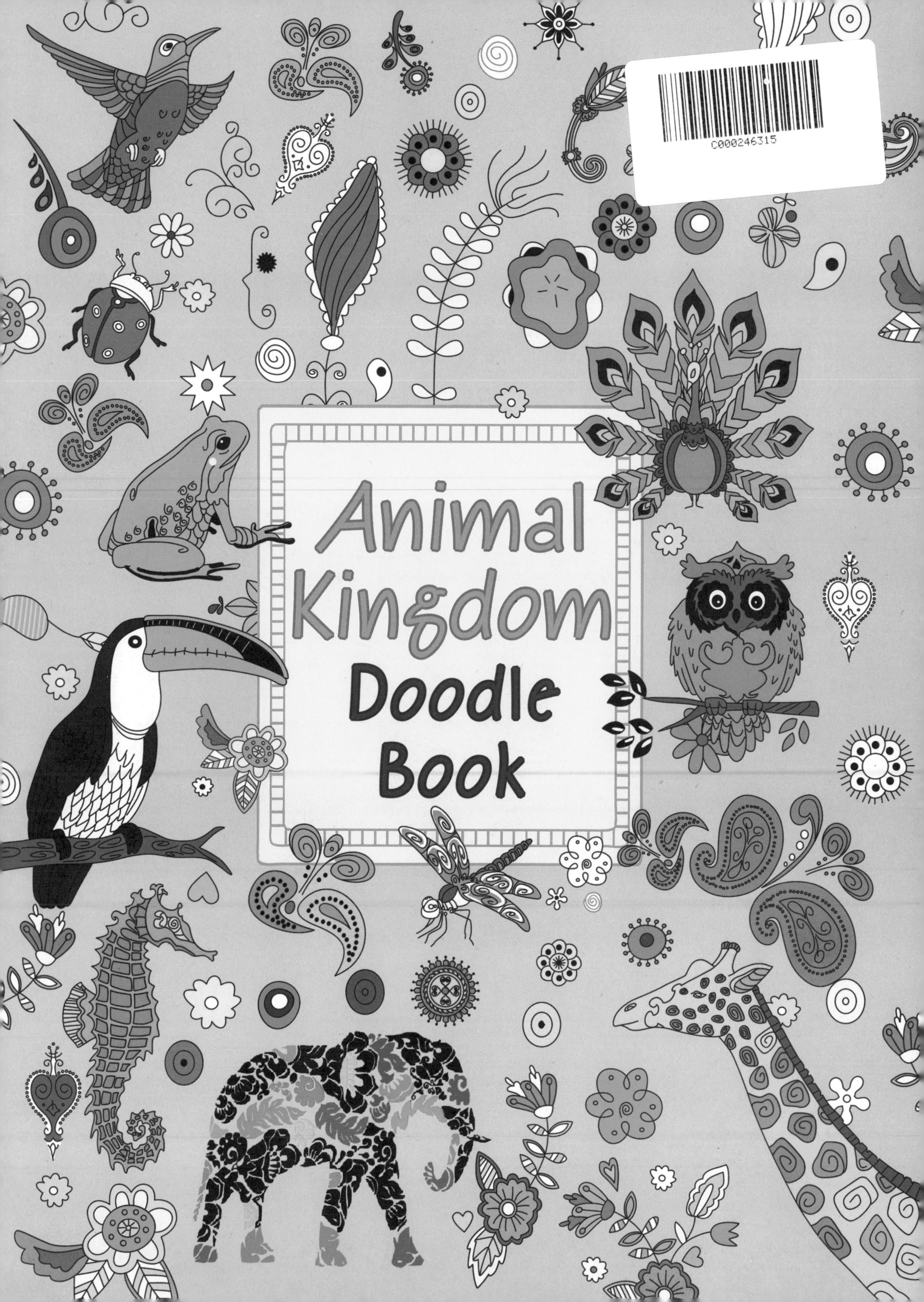

Animal Kingdom Doodle Book

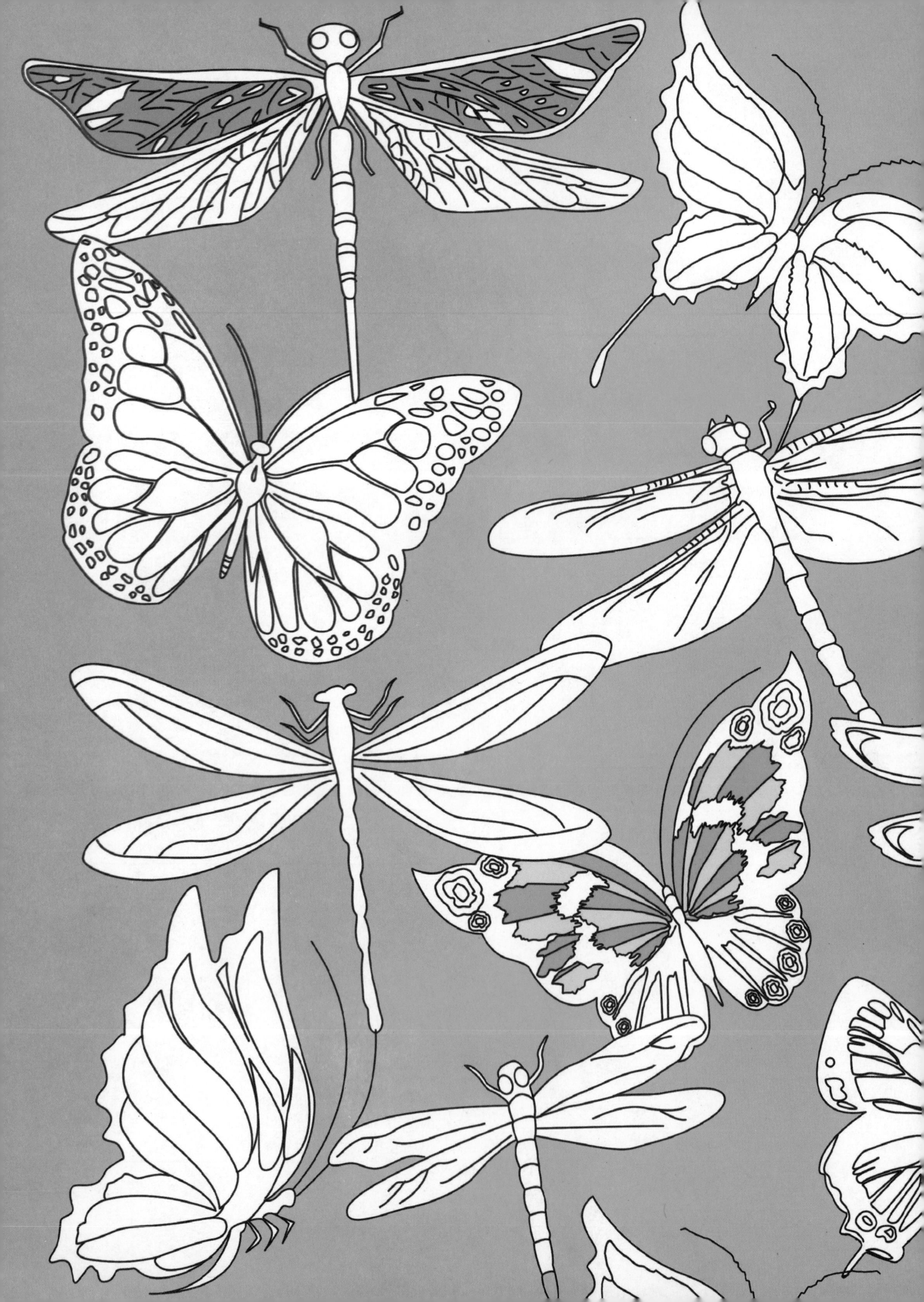

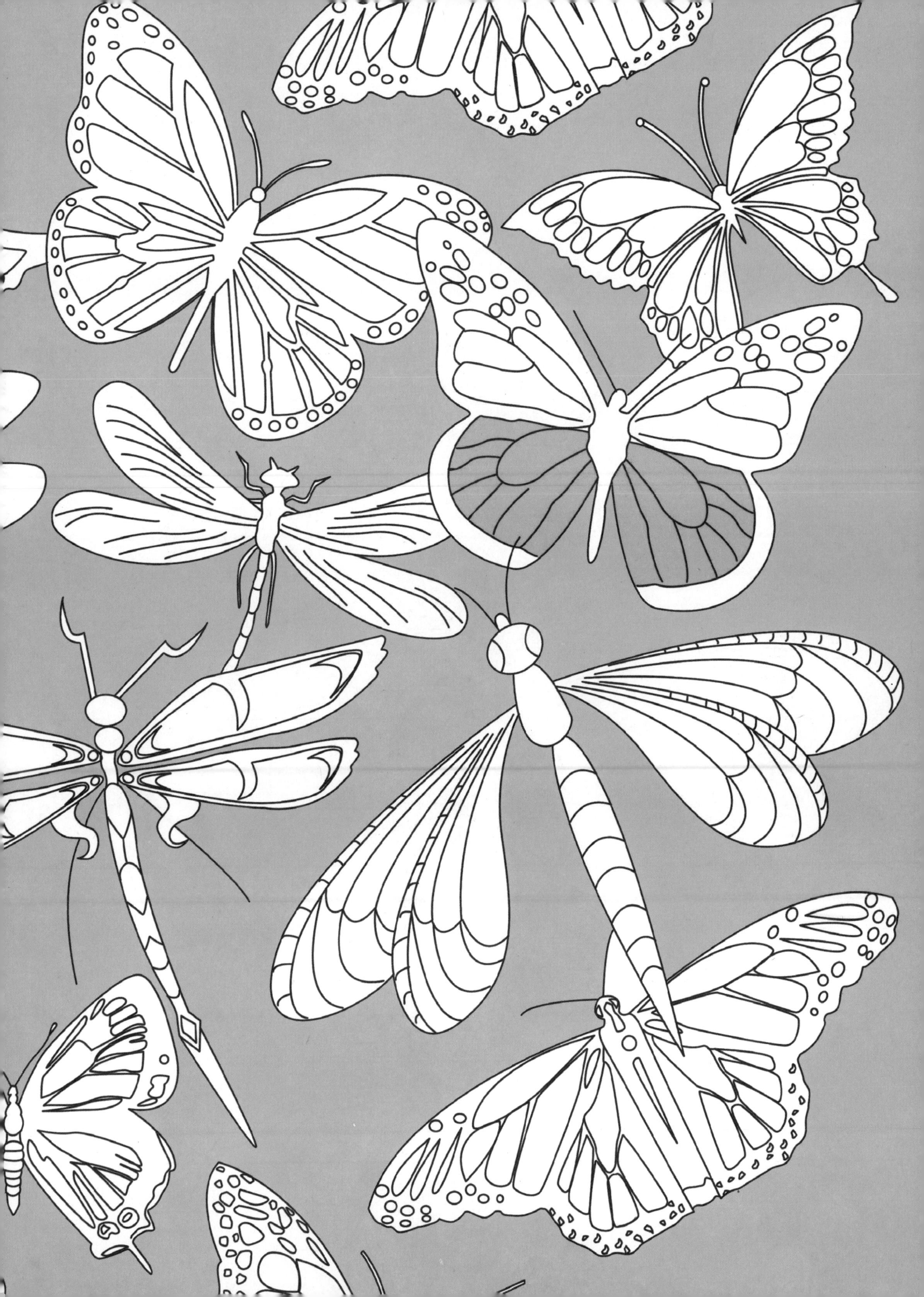

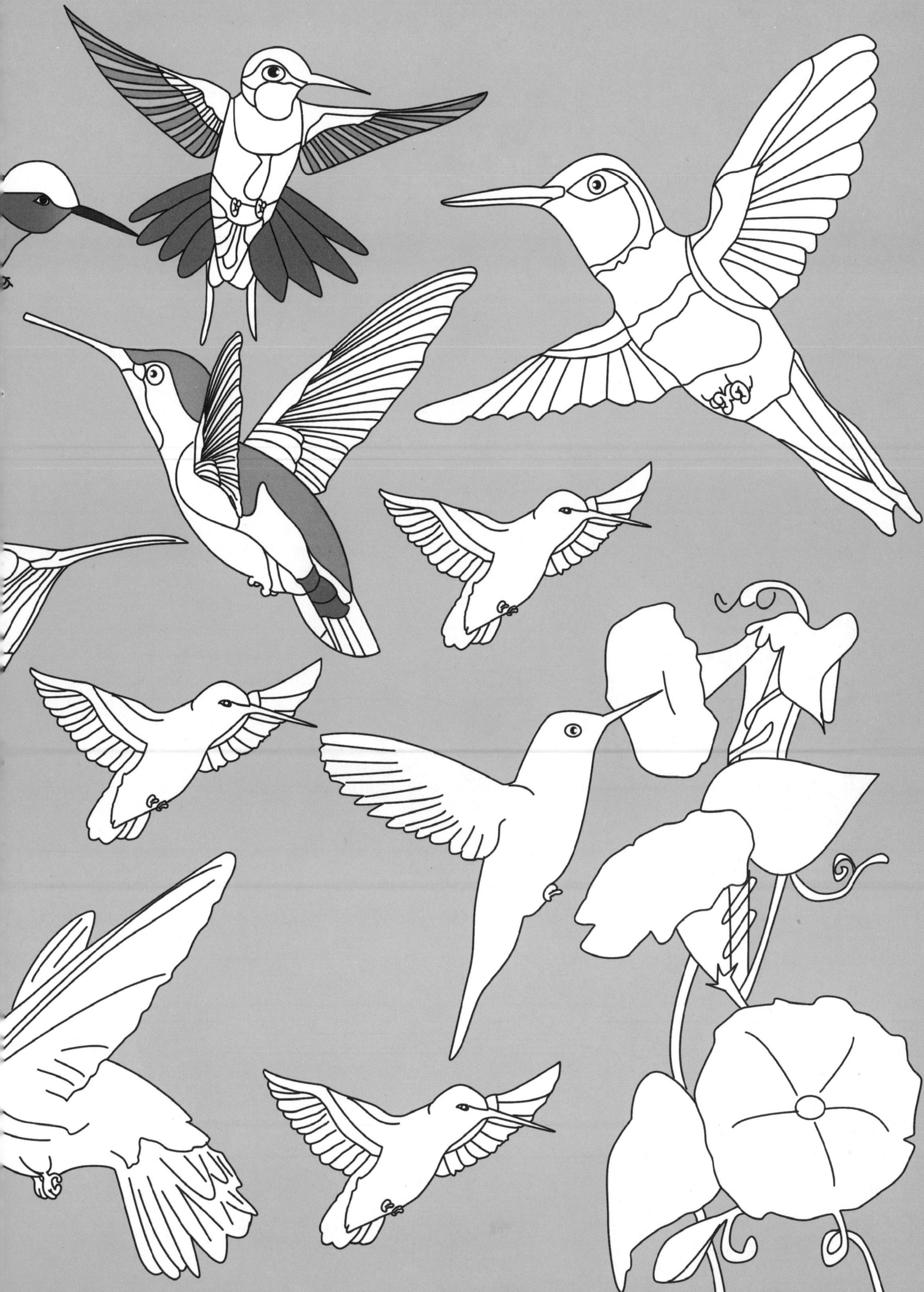

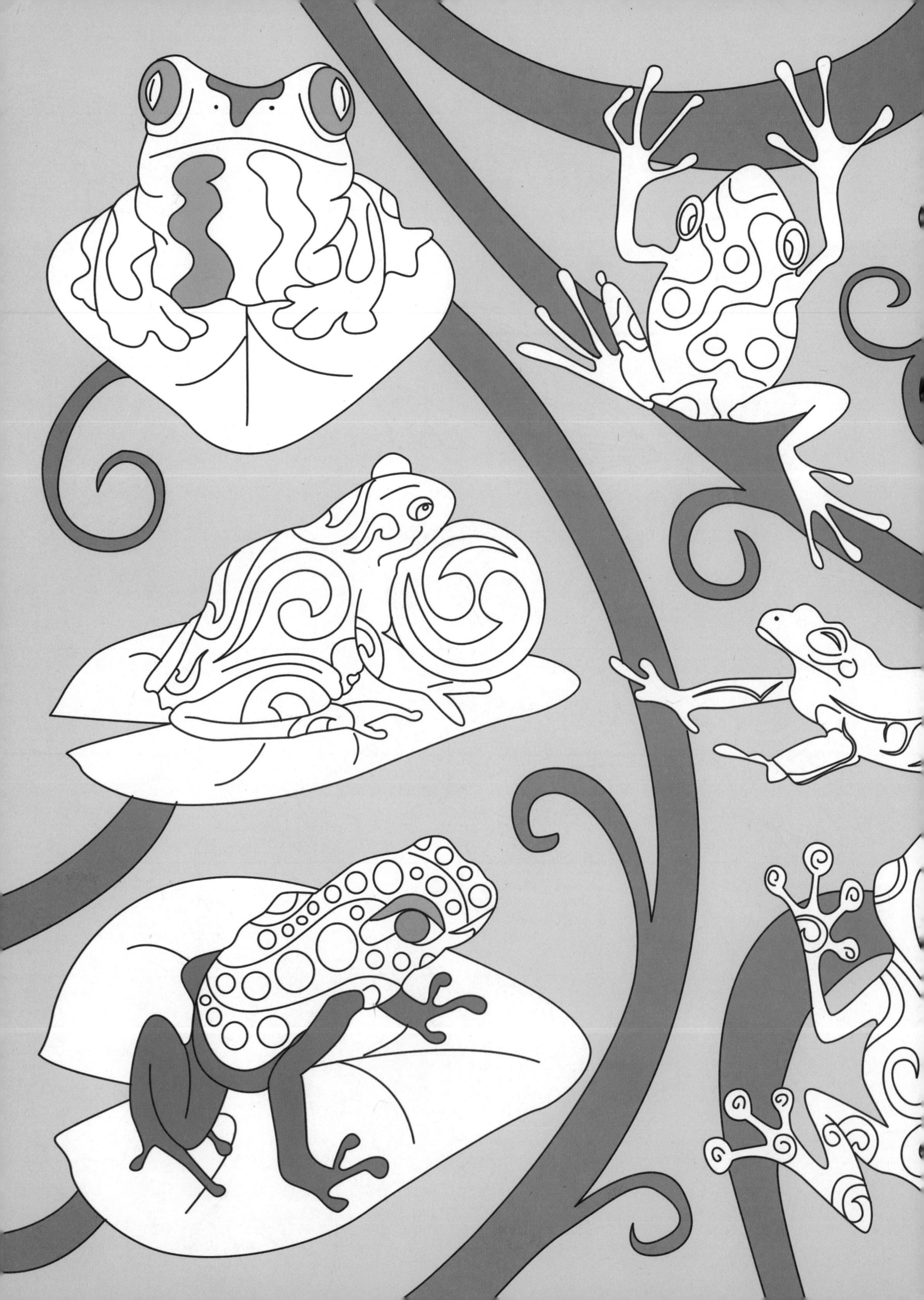

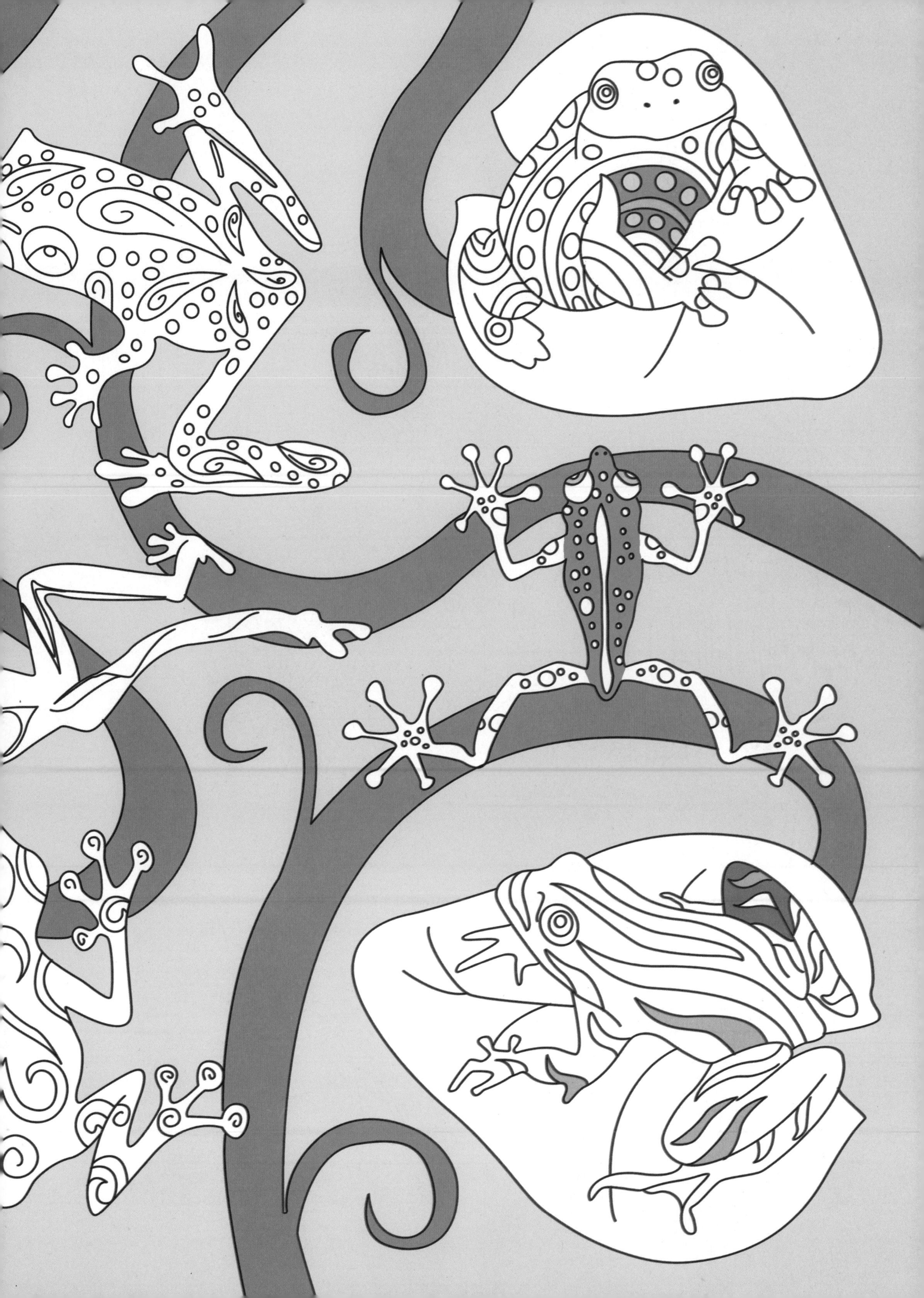

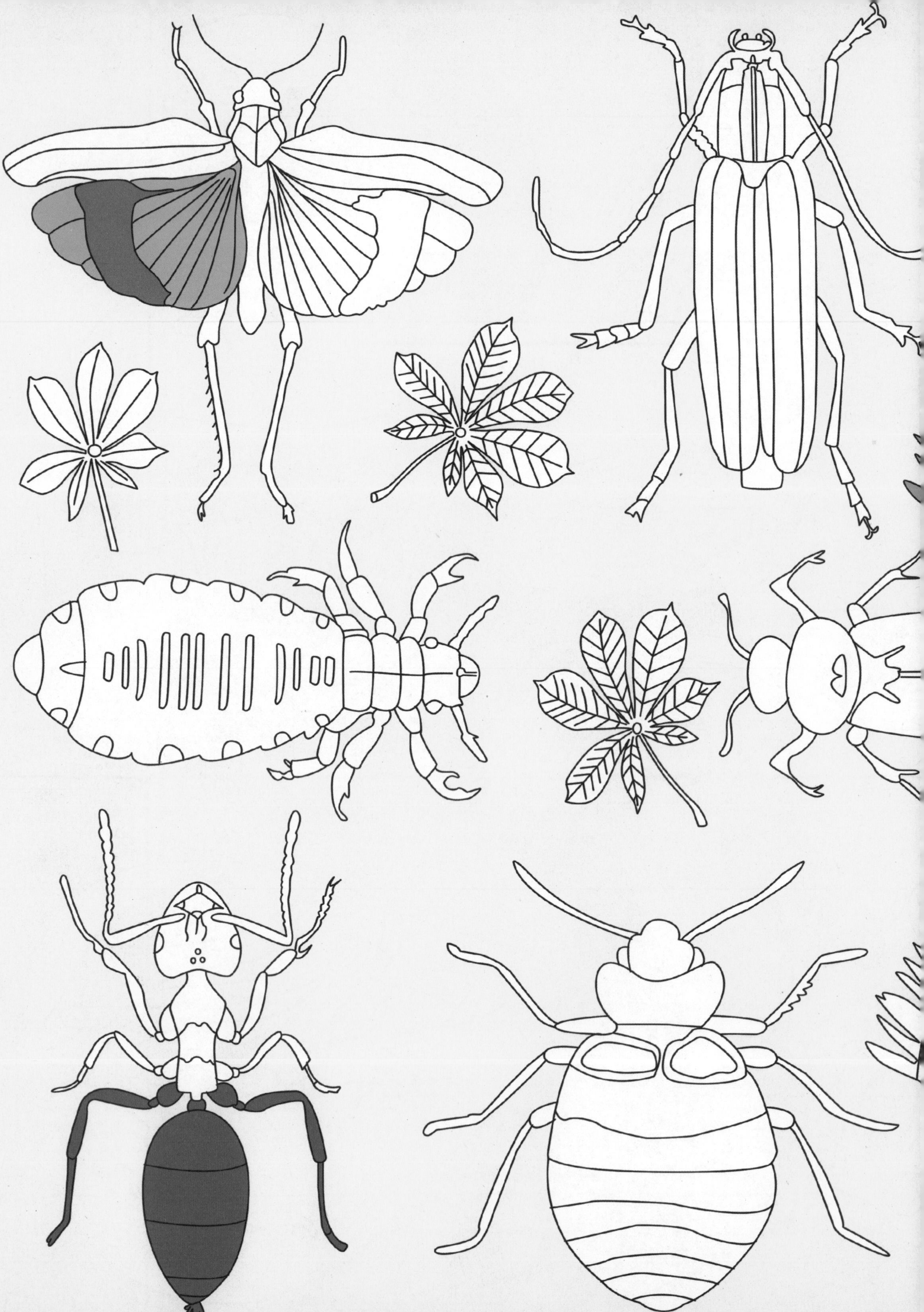

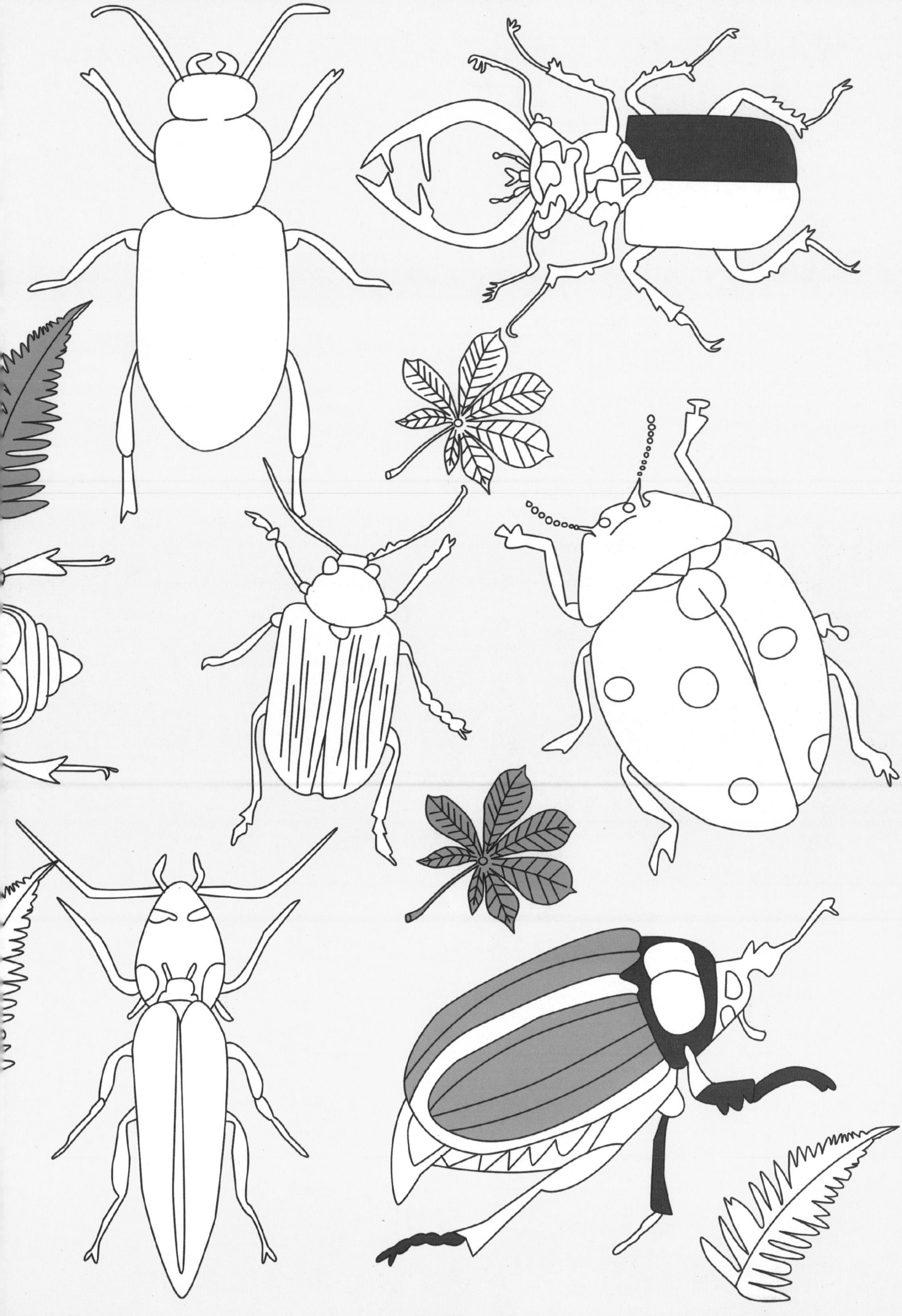

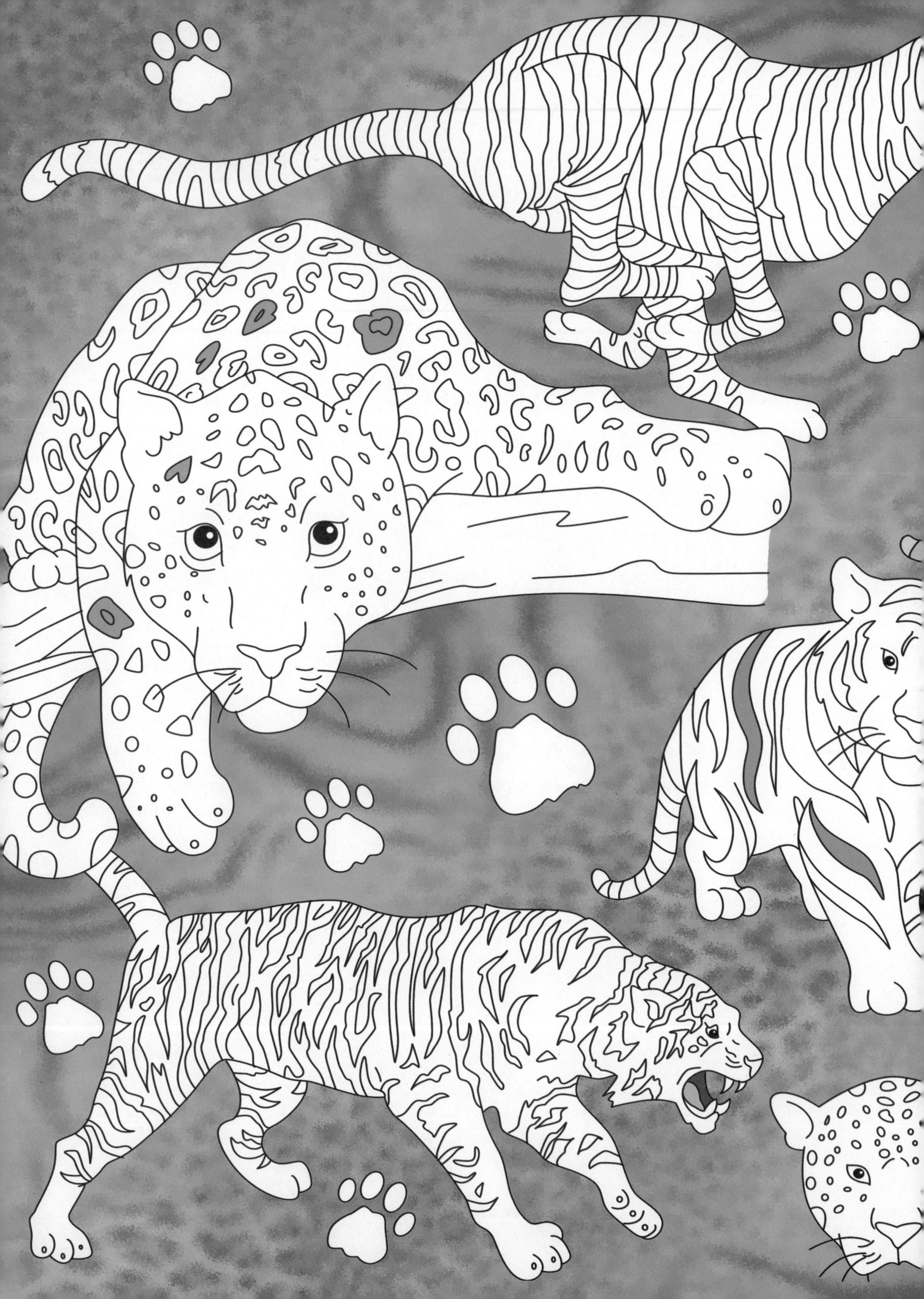

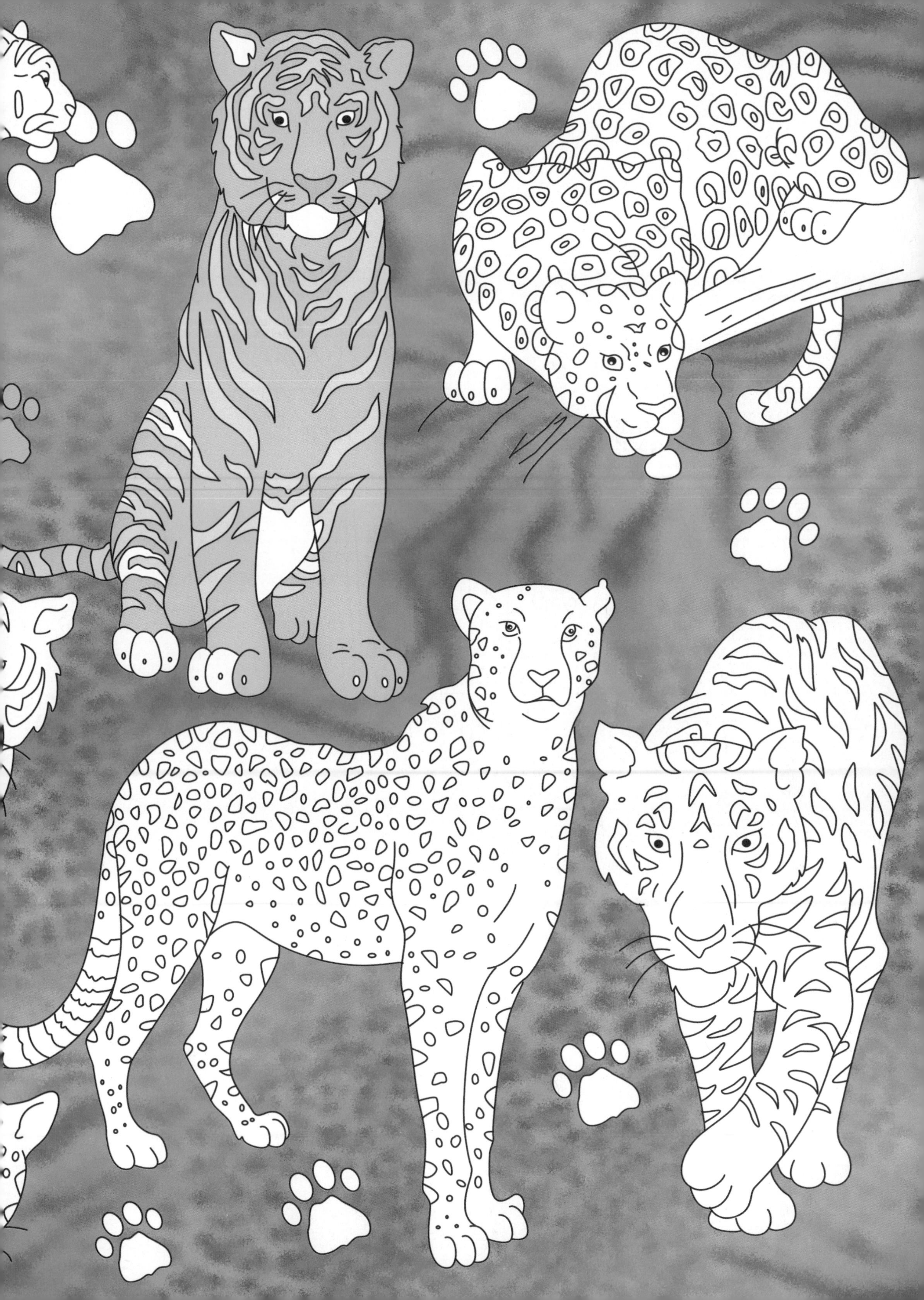

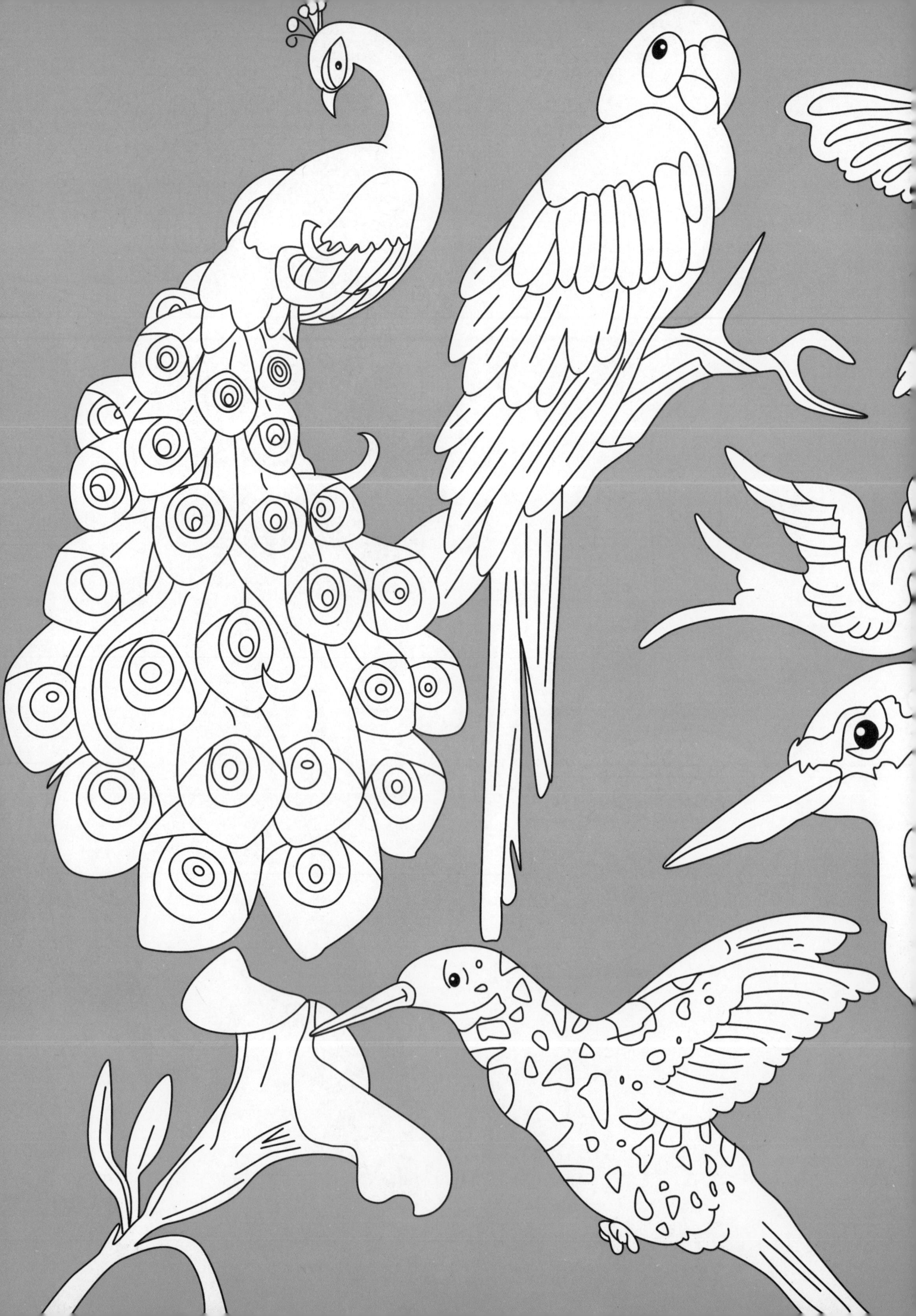

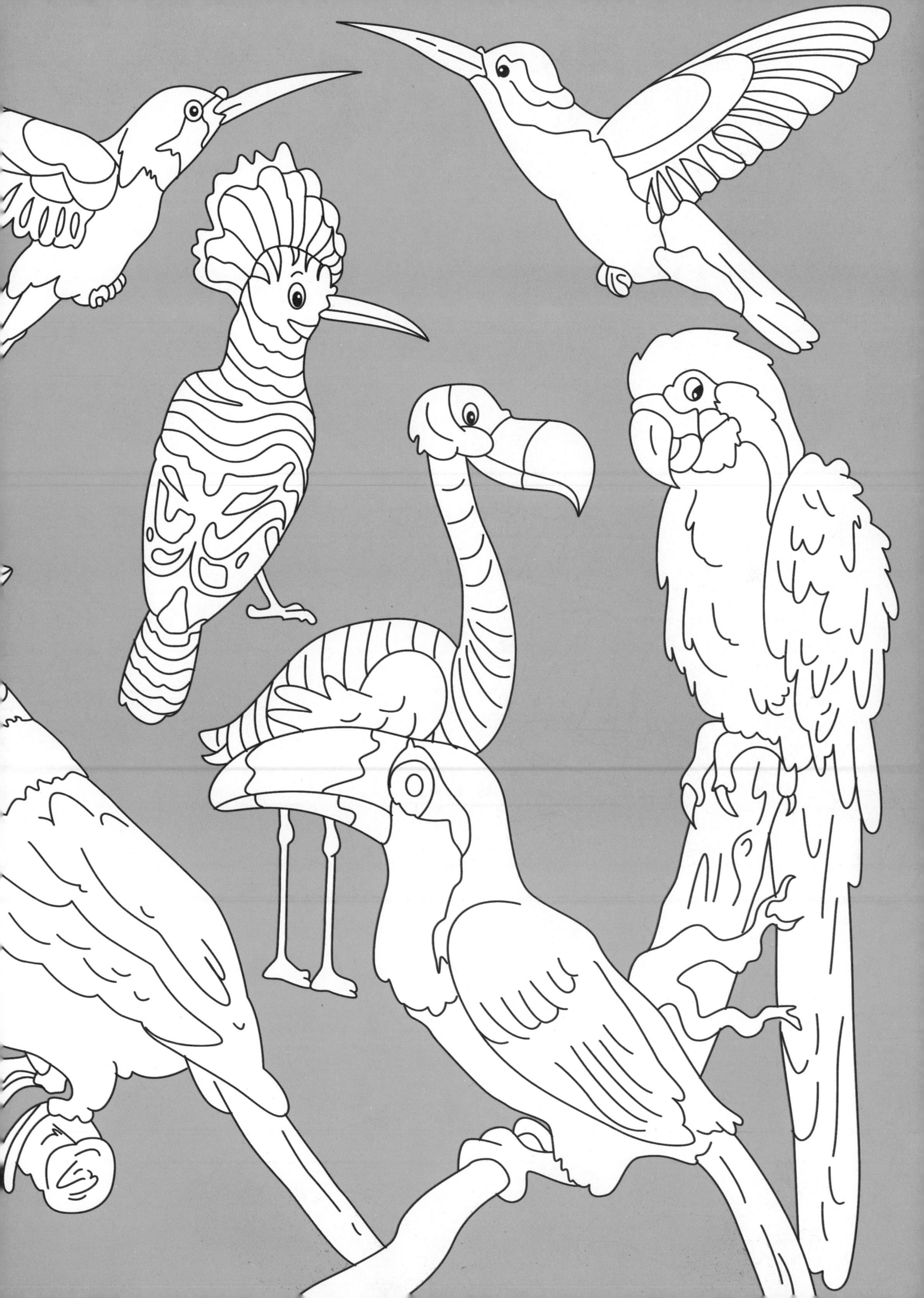

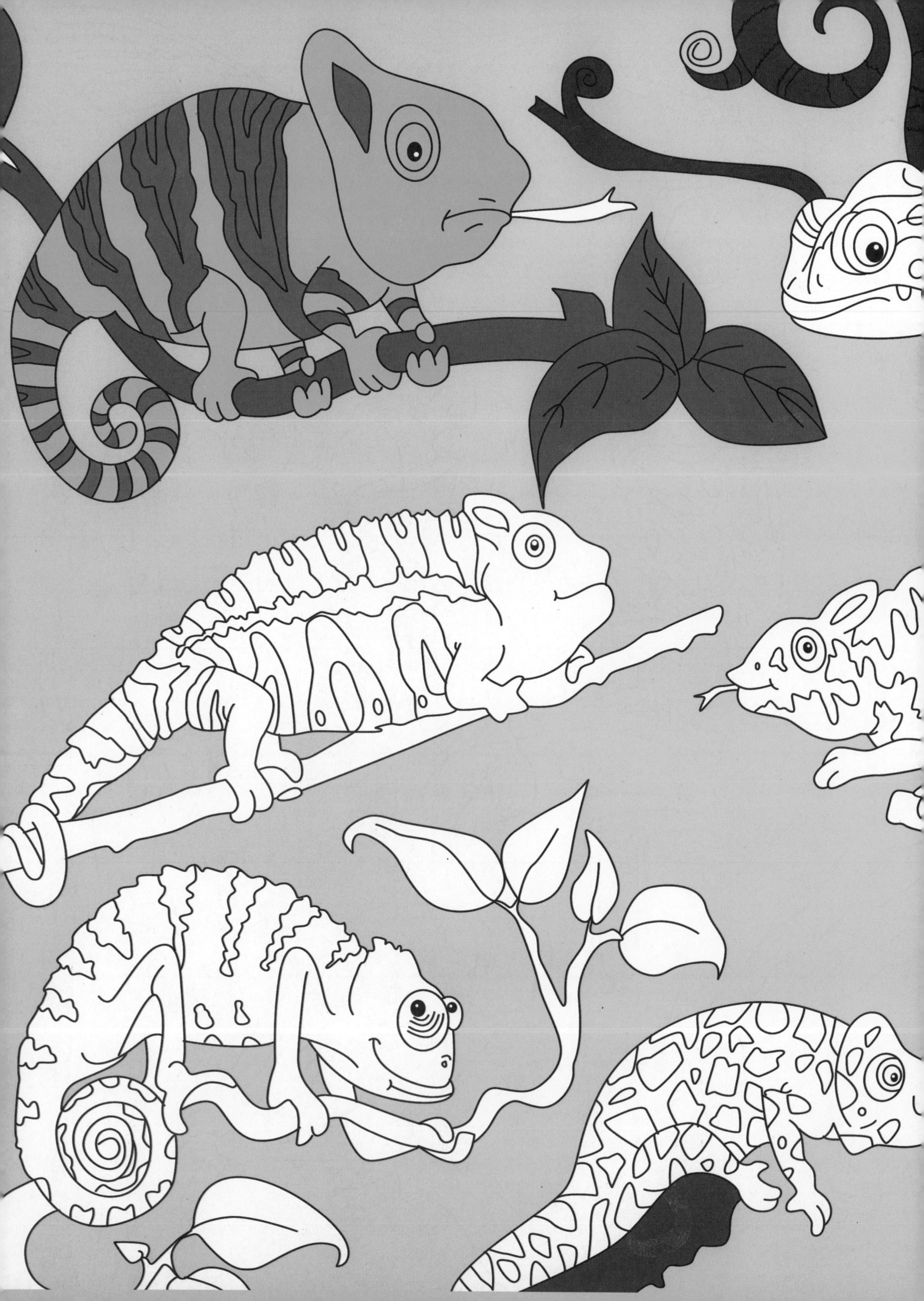

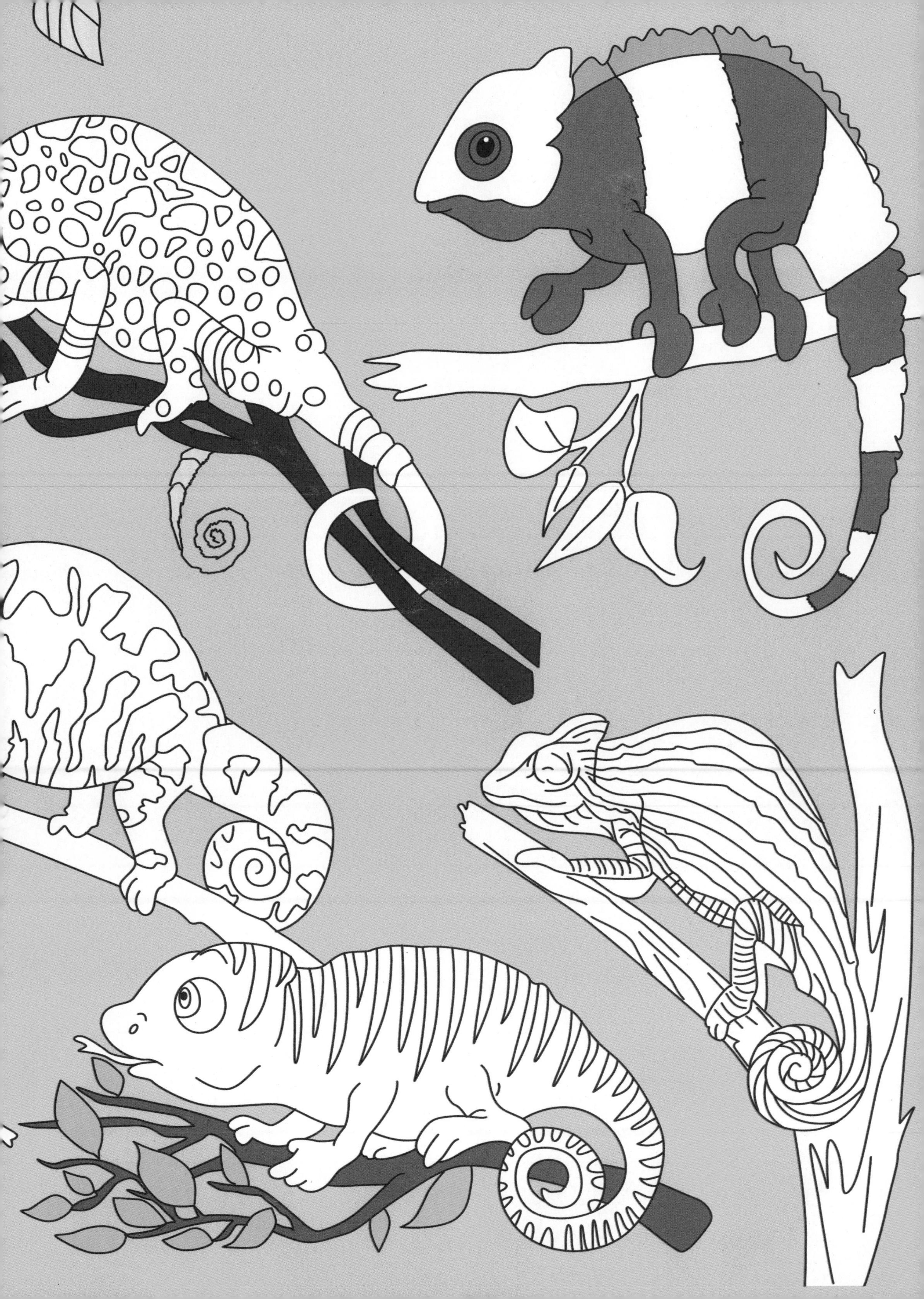

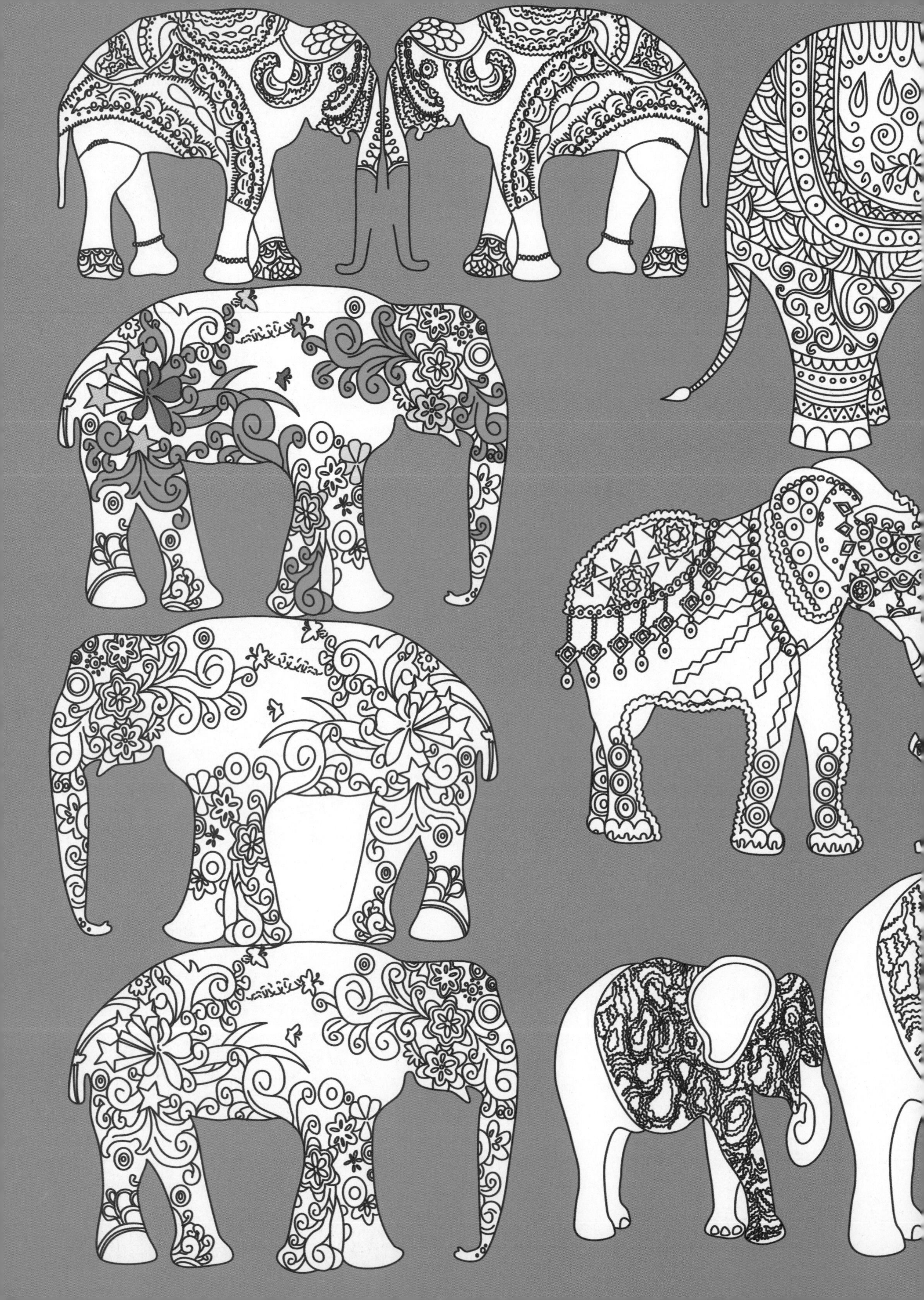

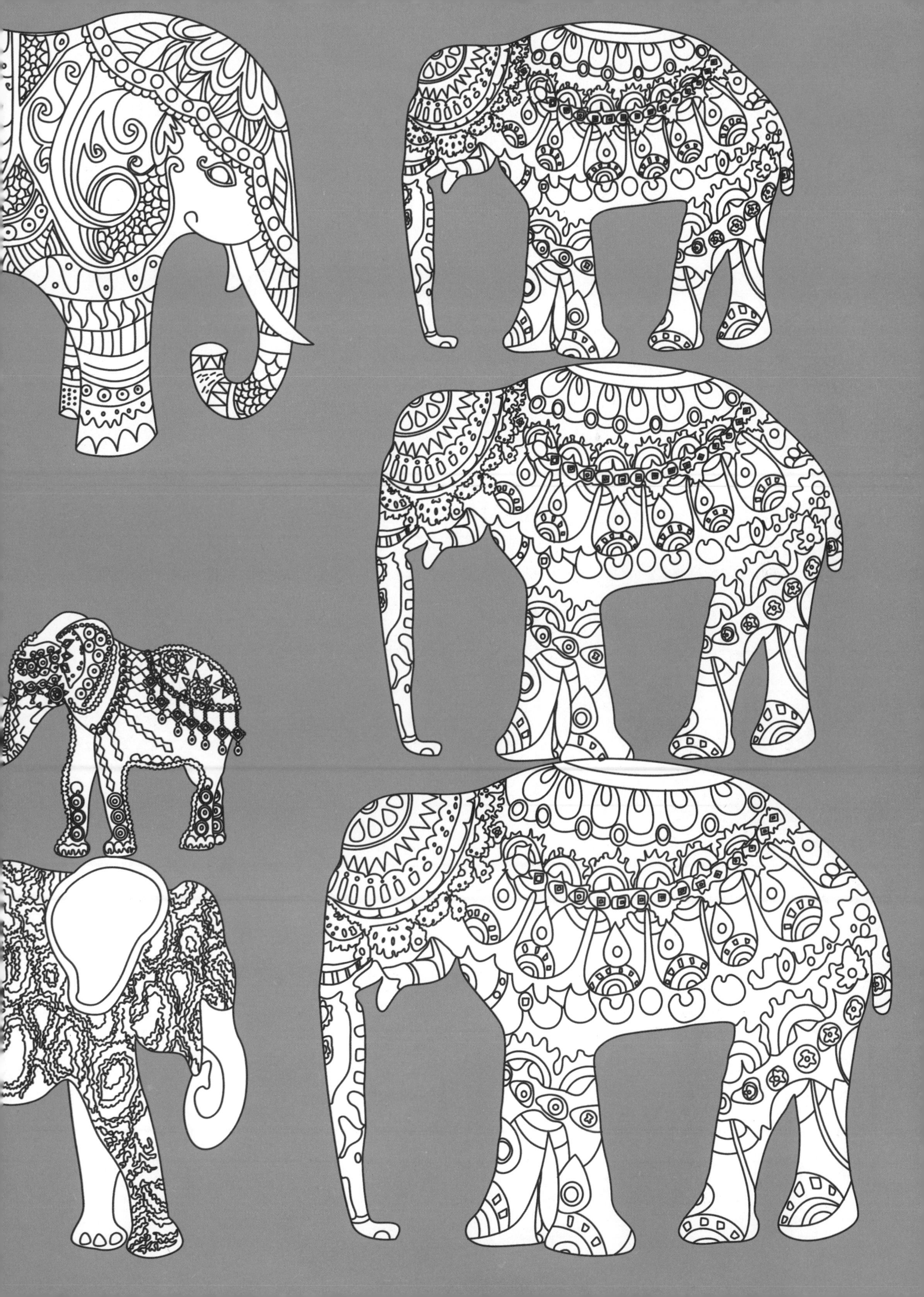

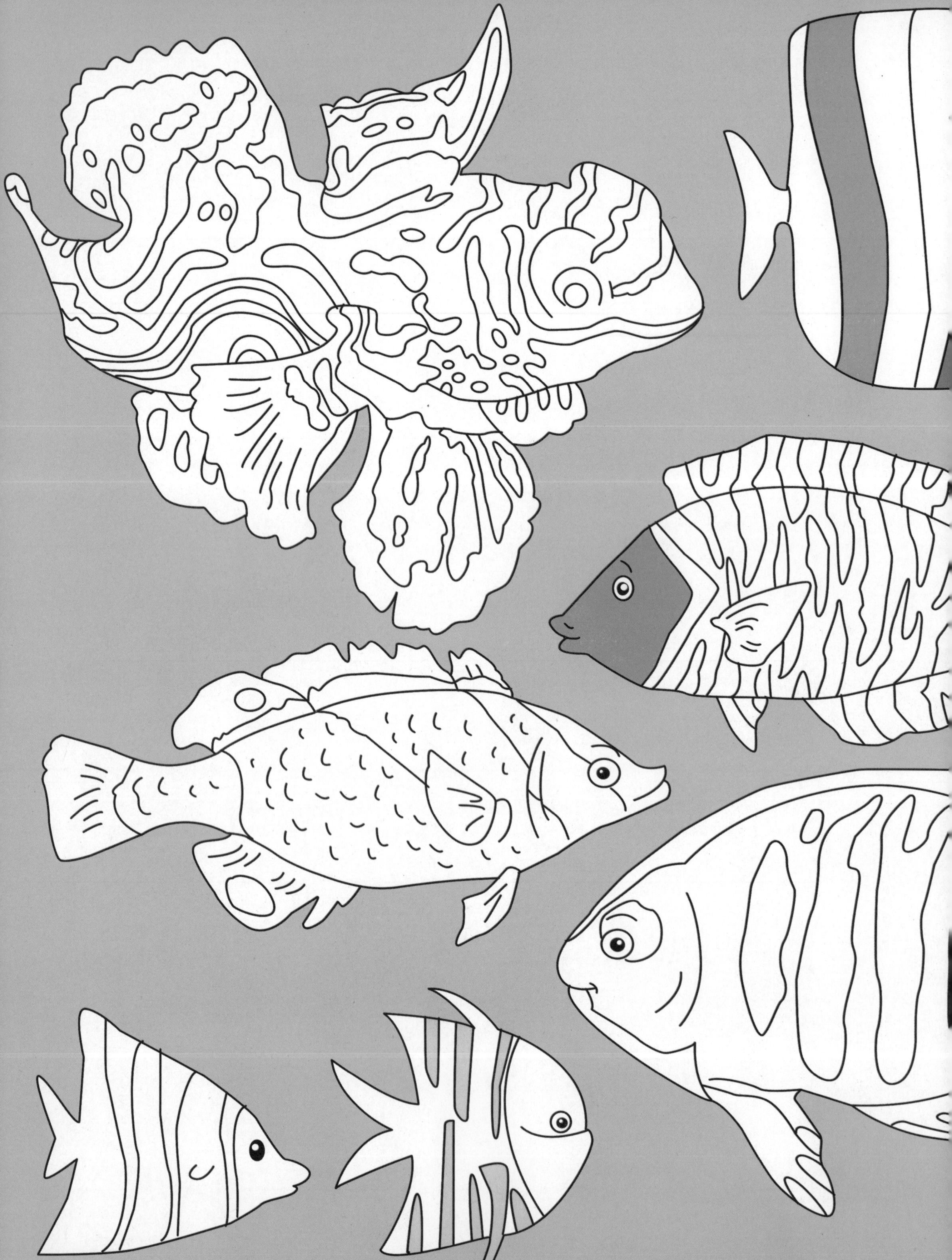

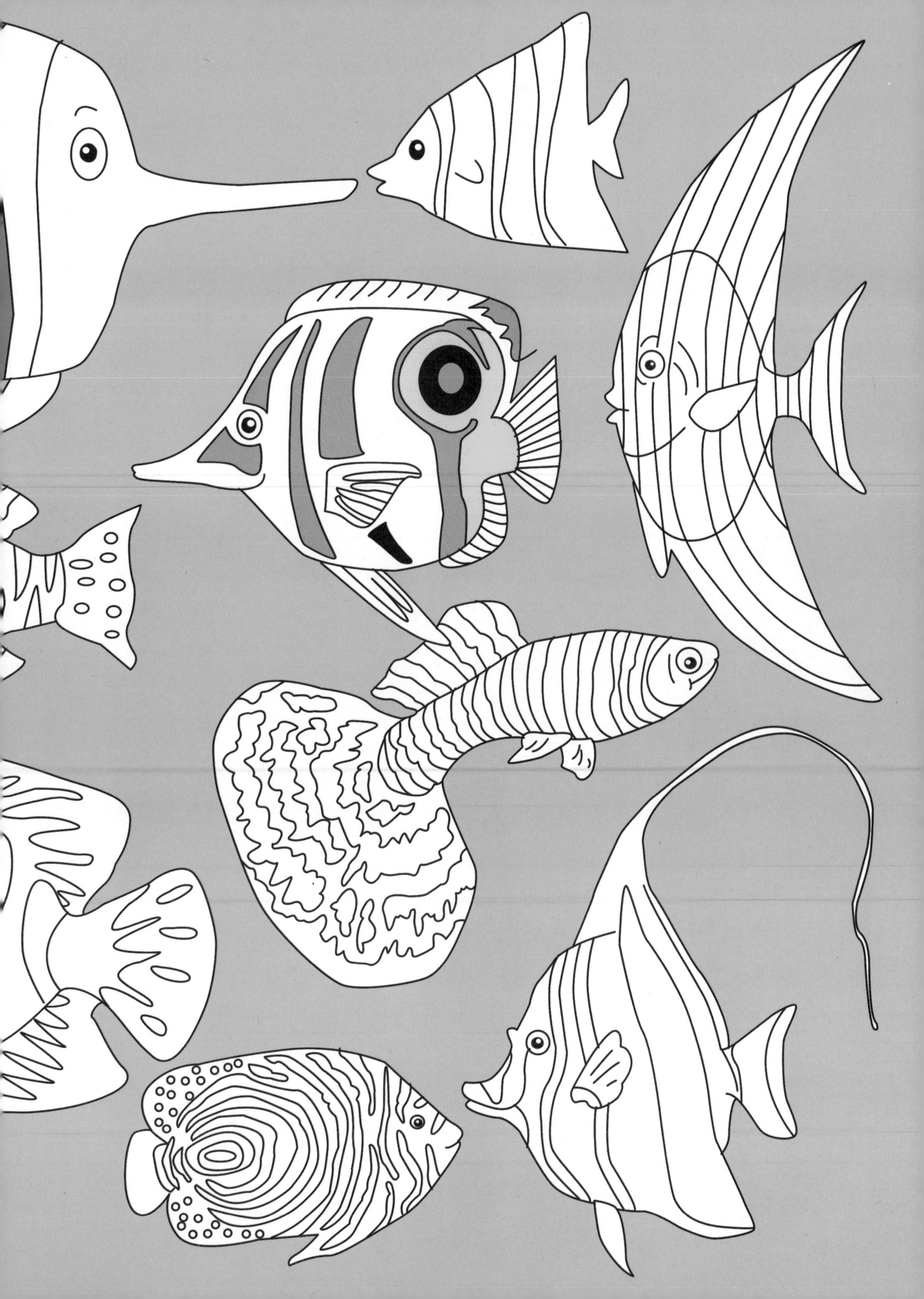

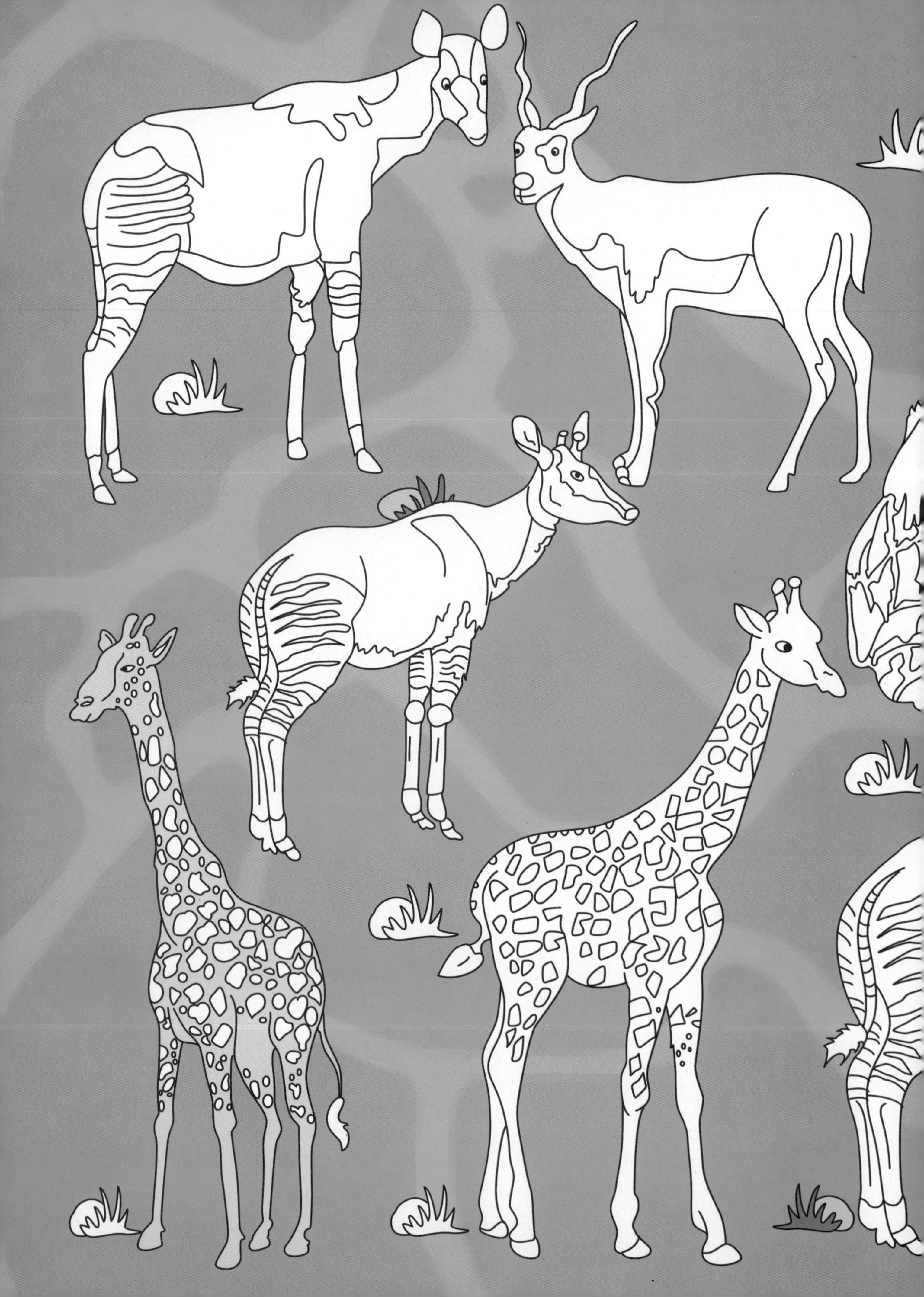

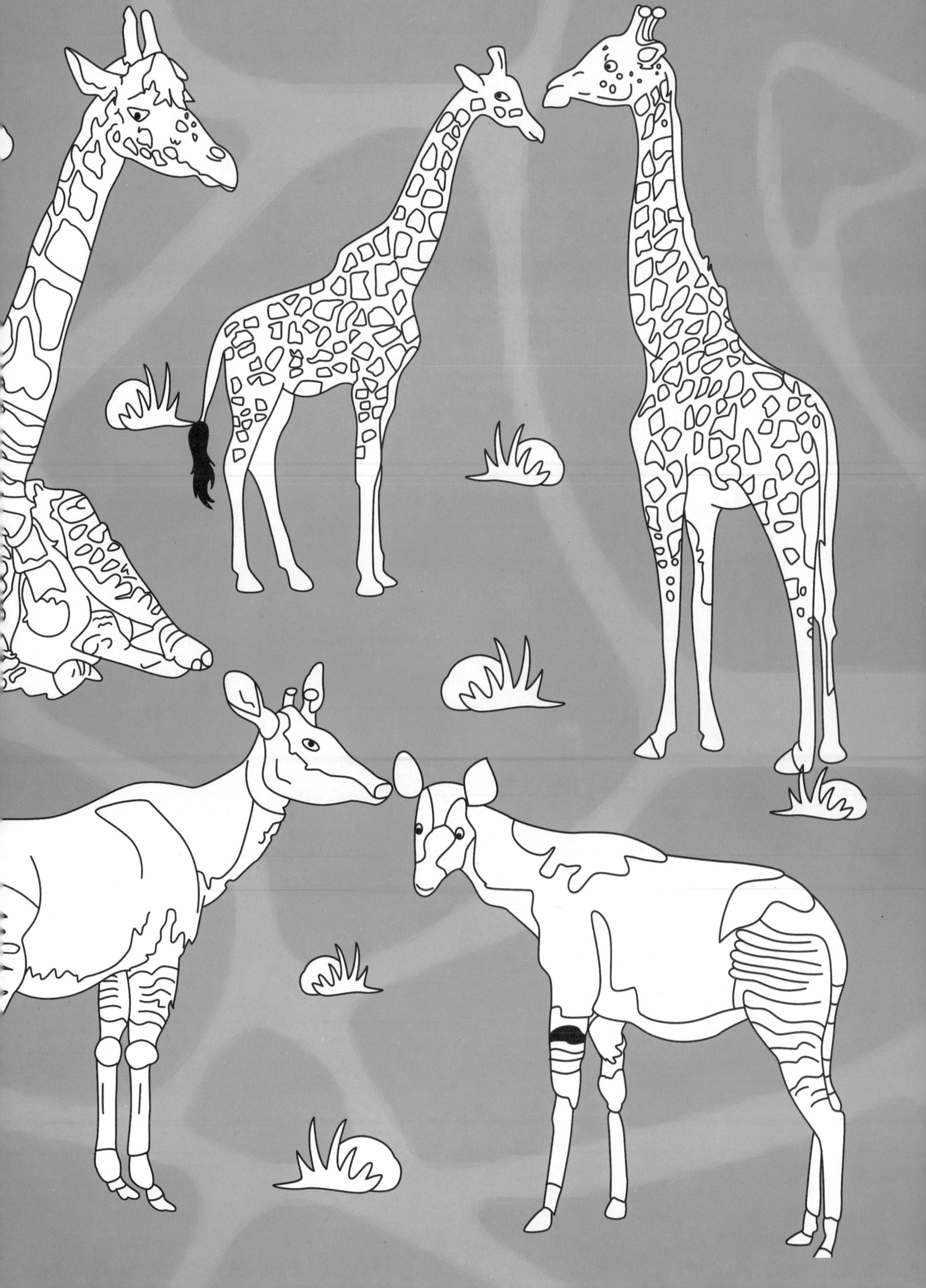

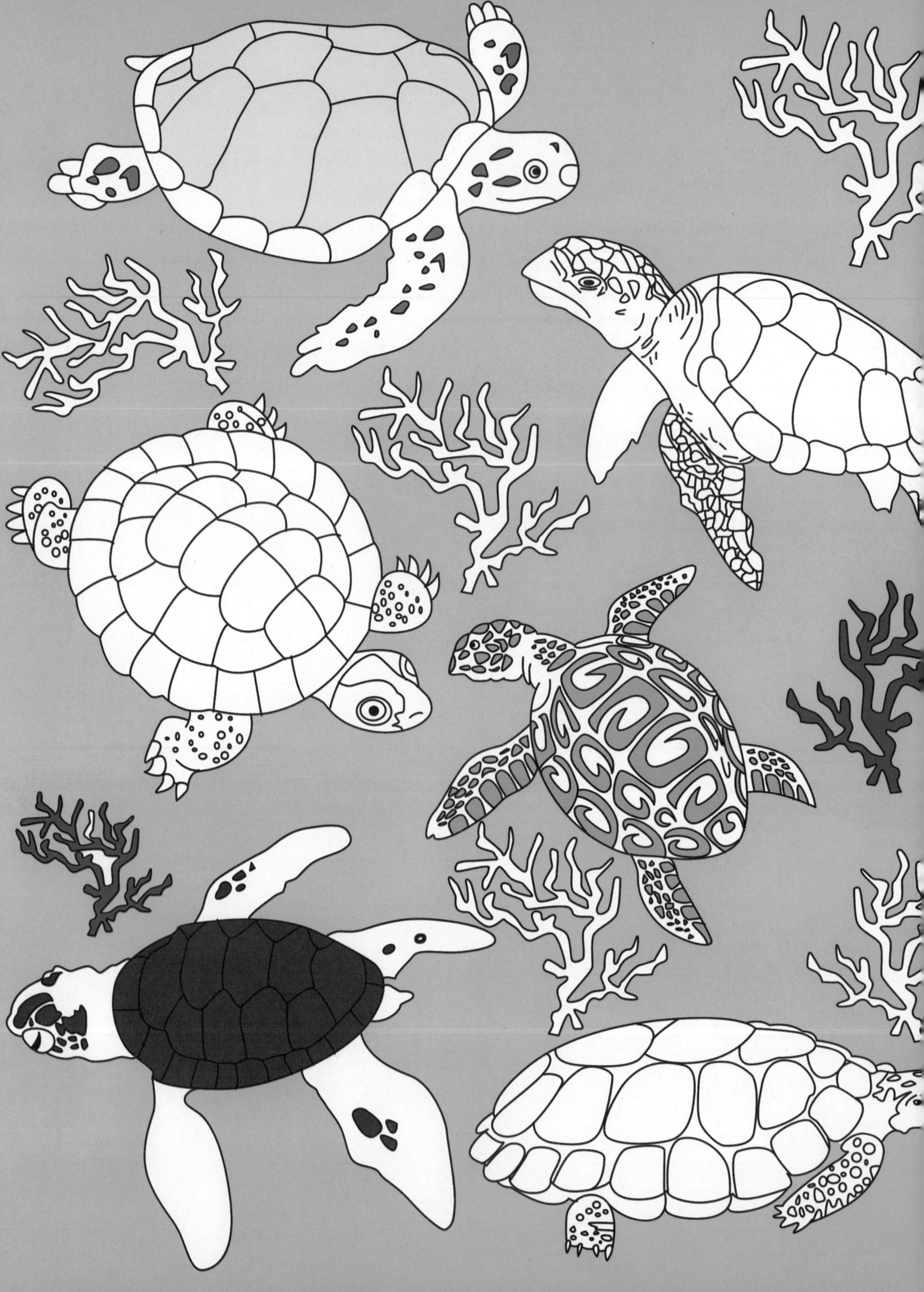

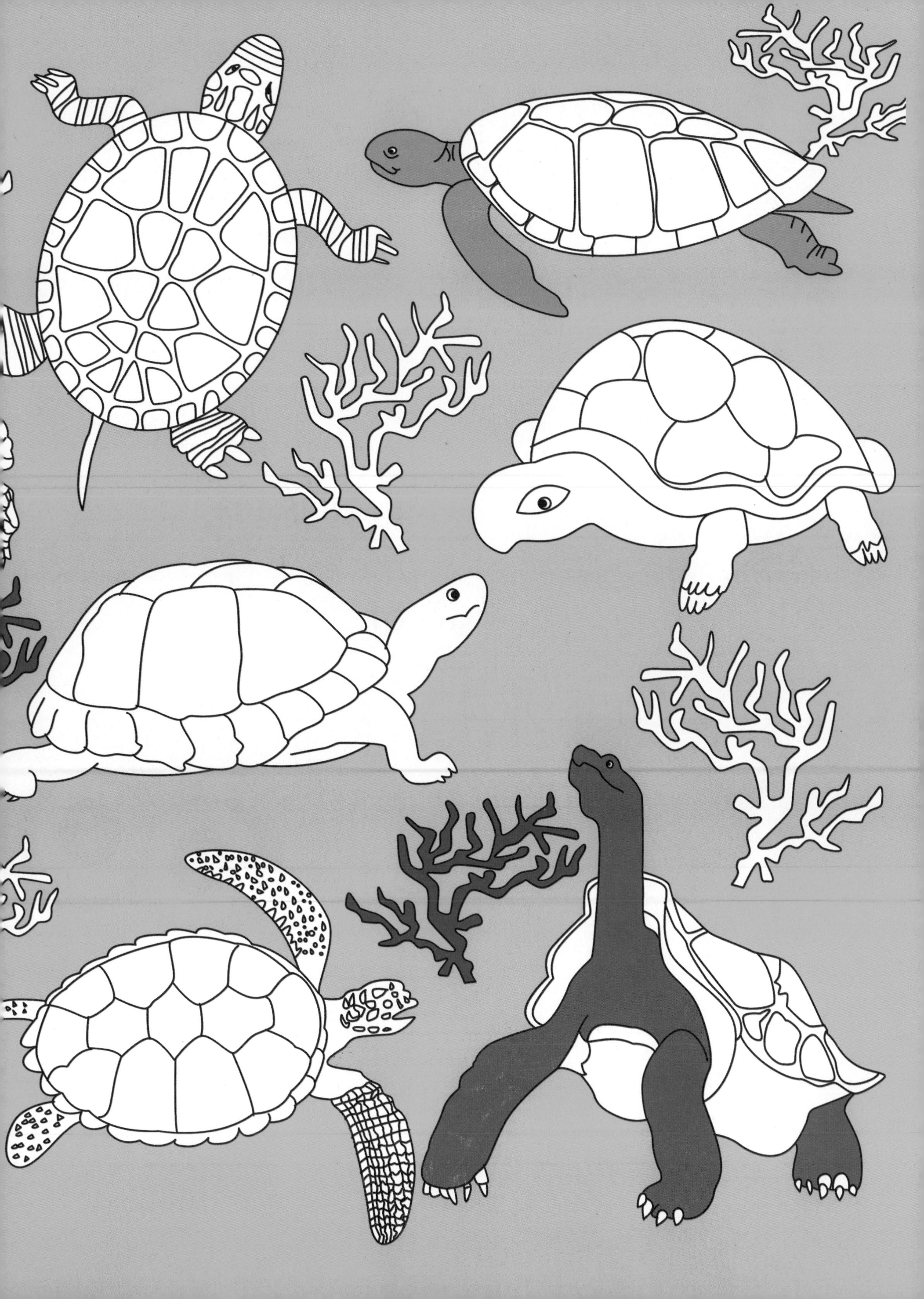

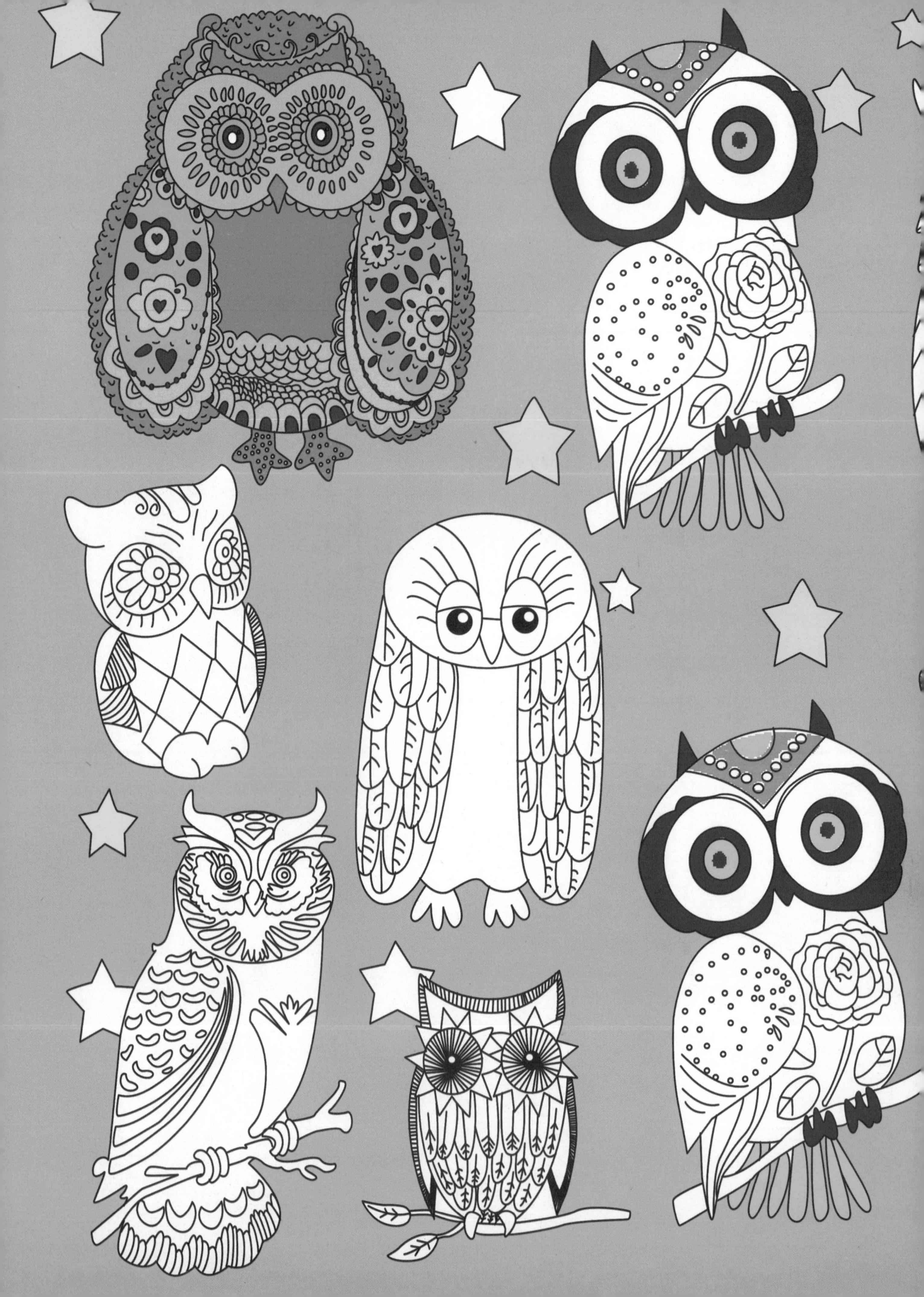

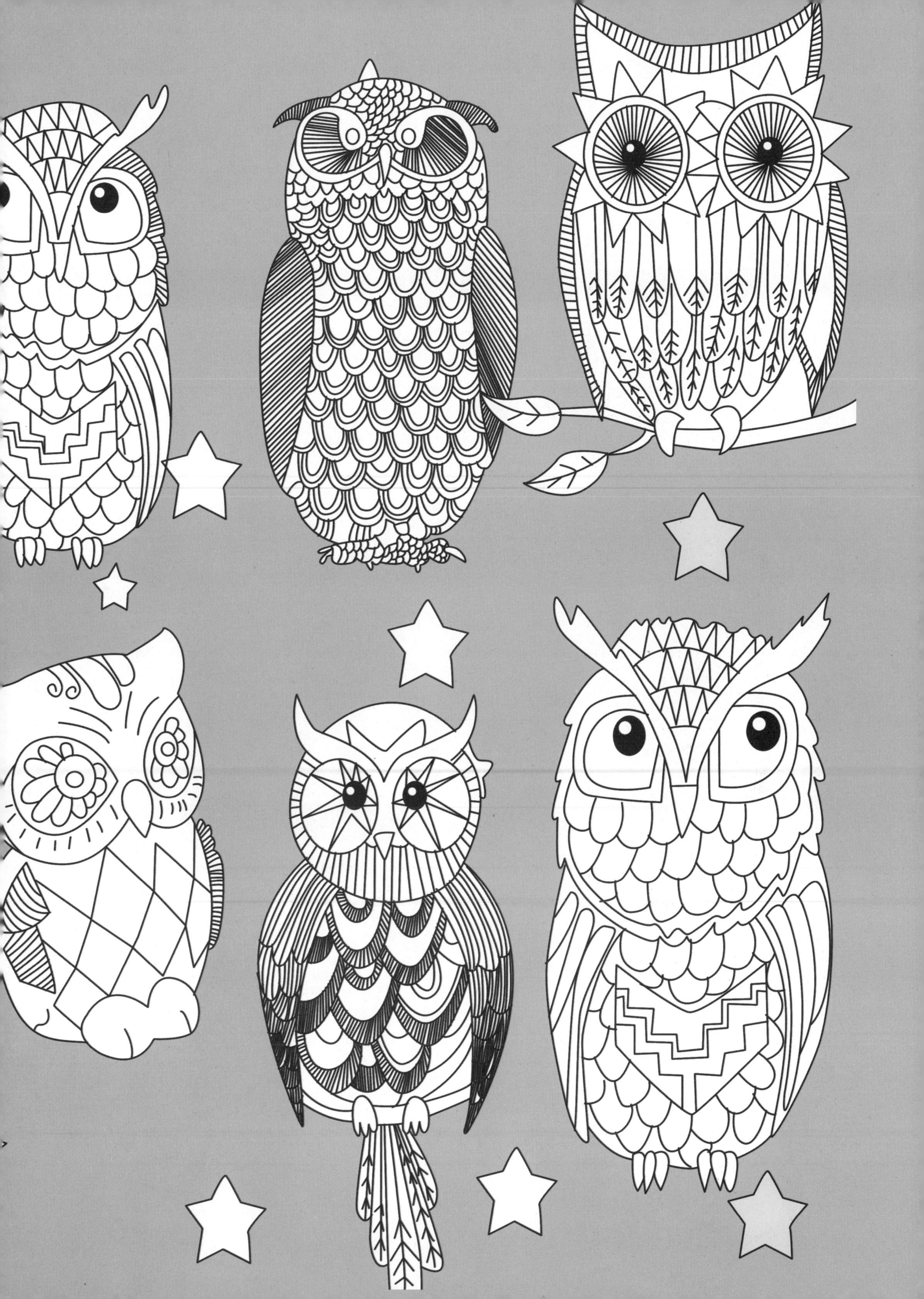

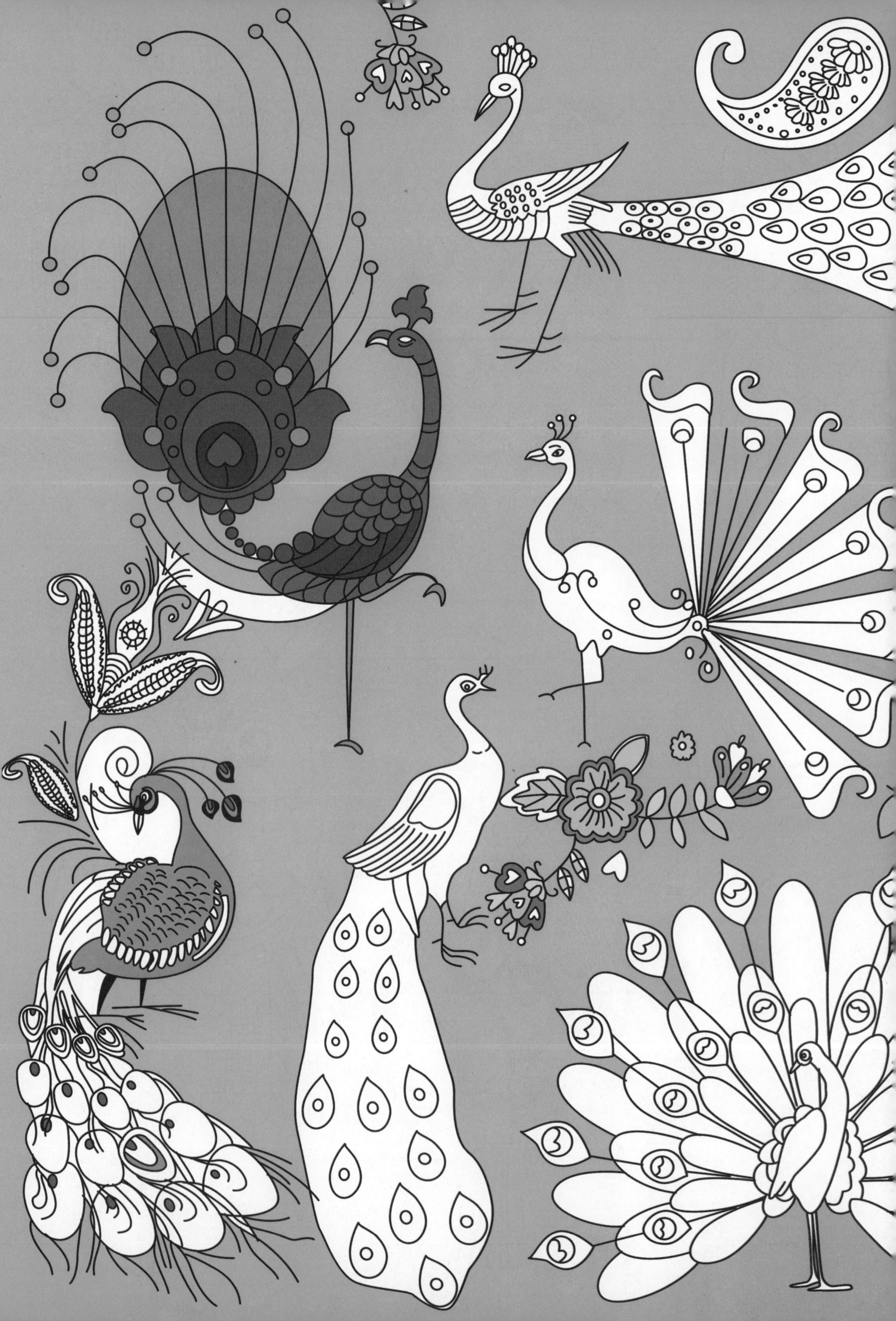

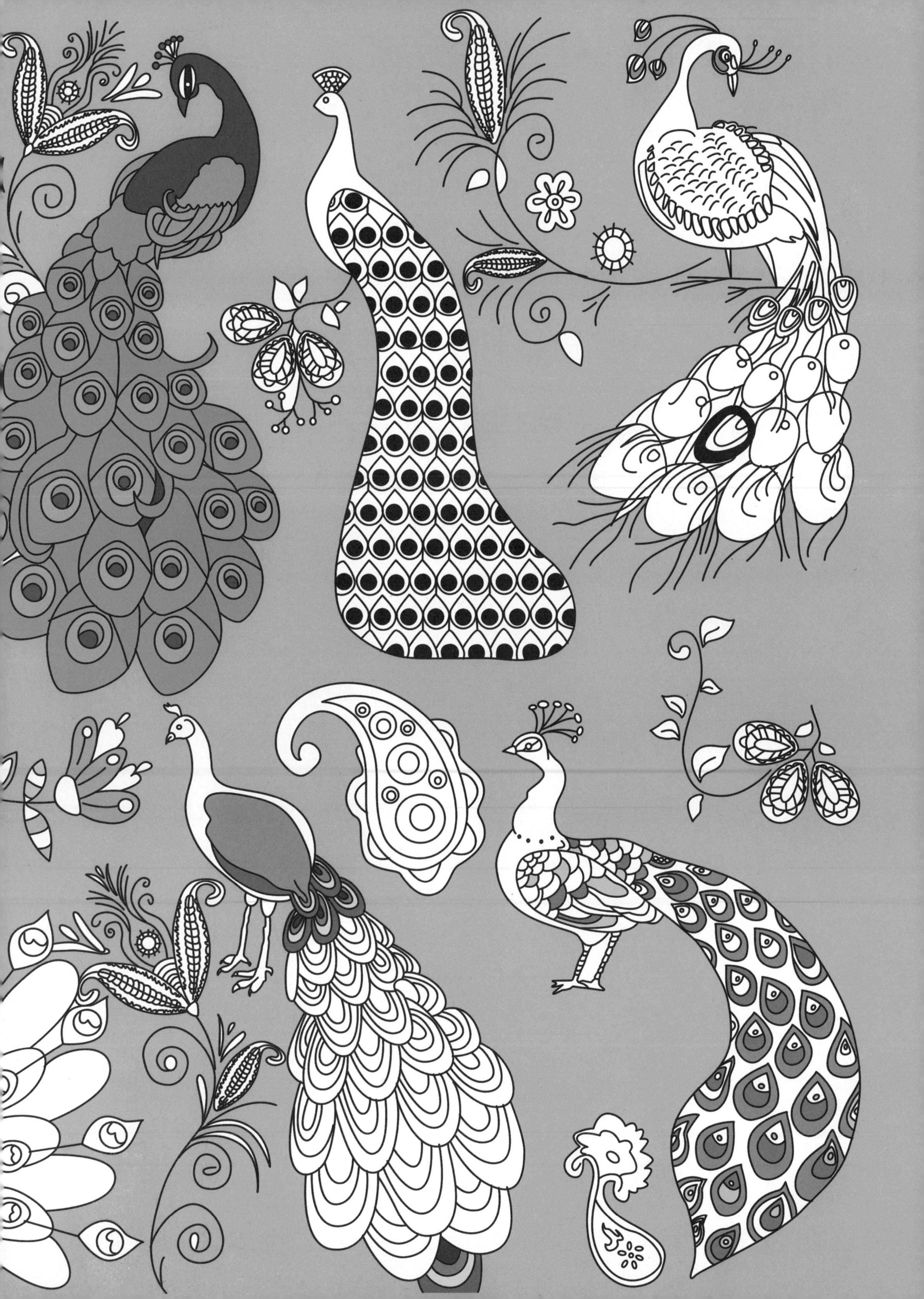

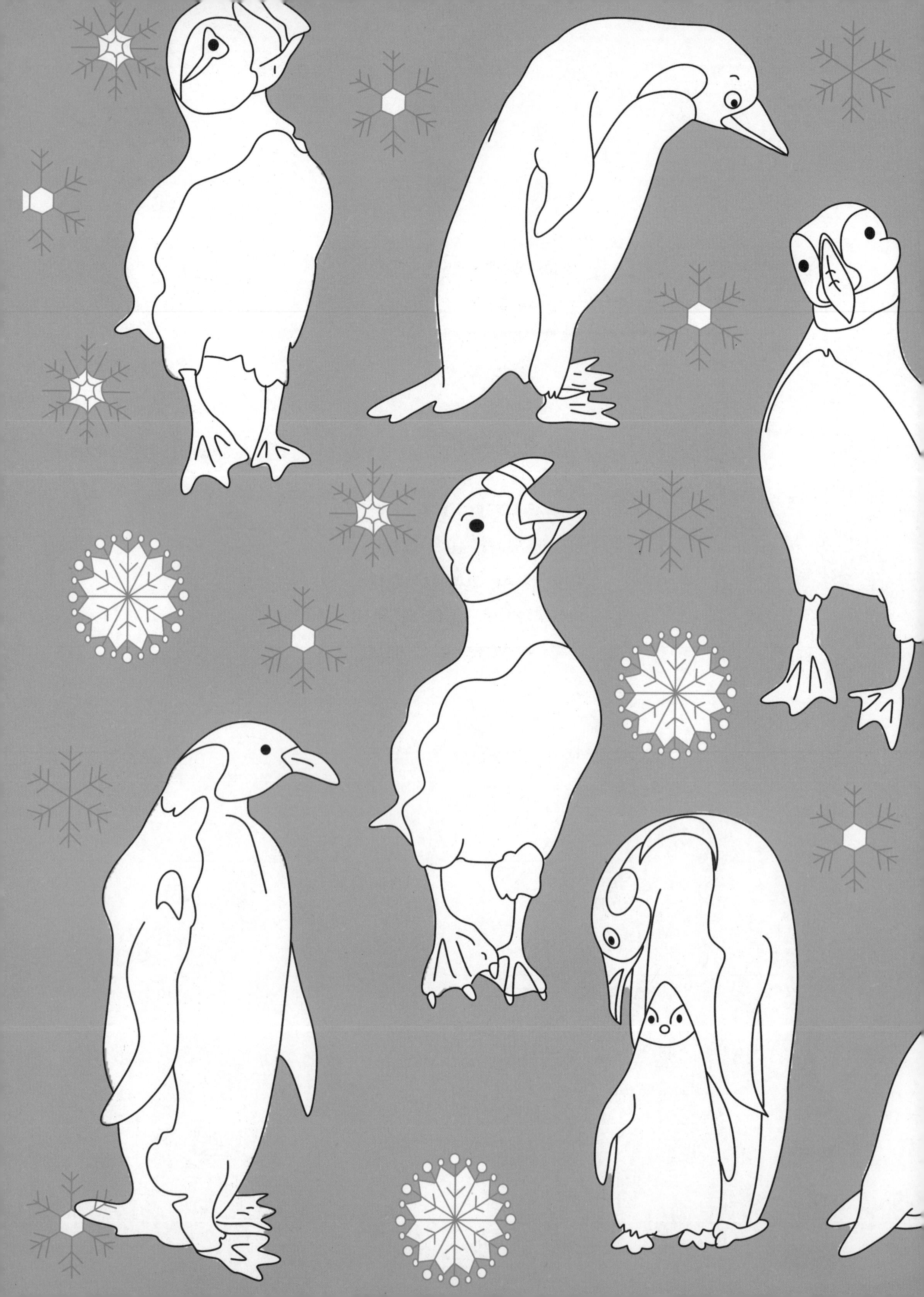

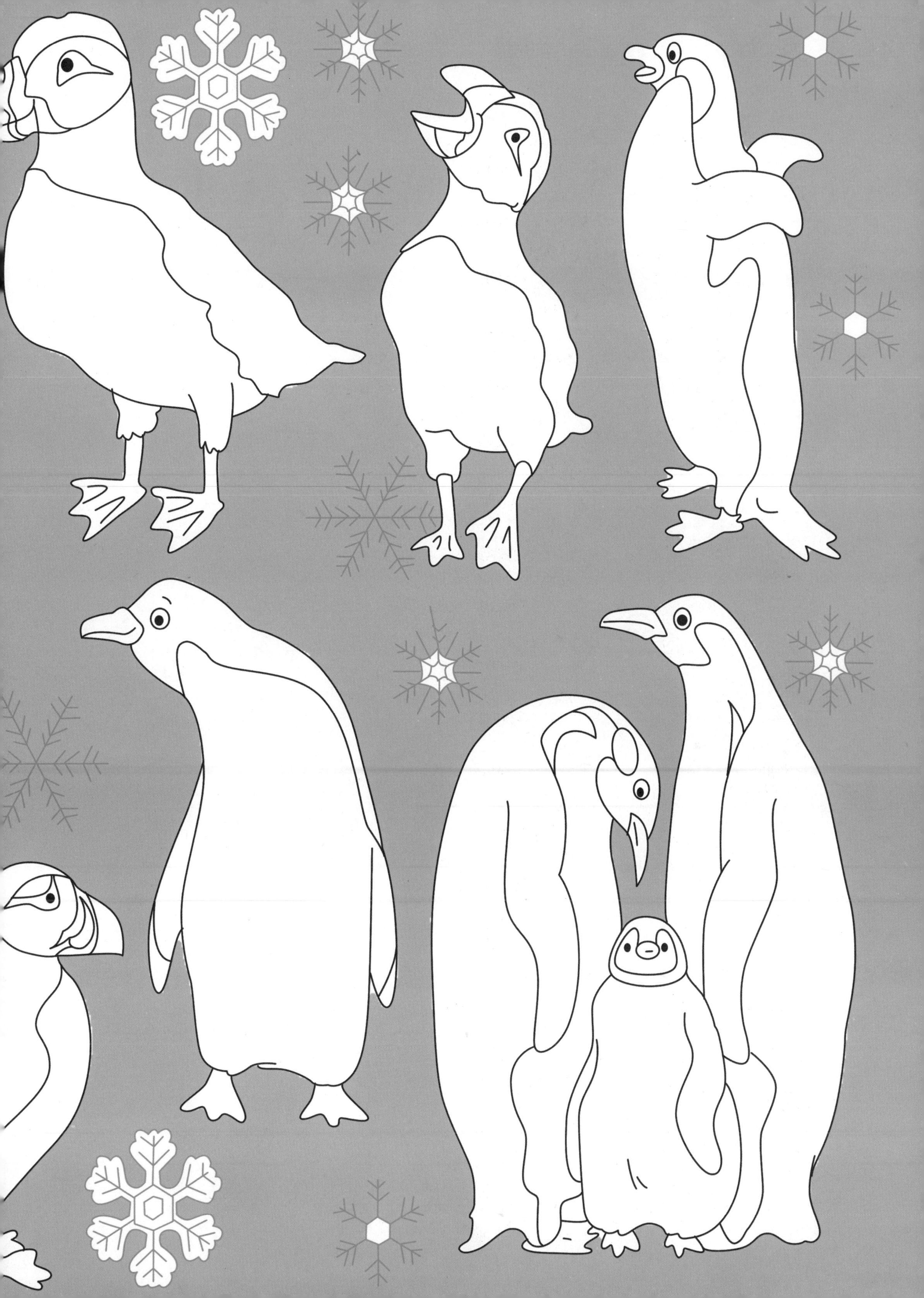

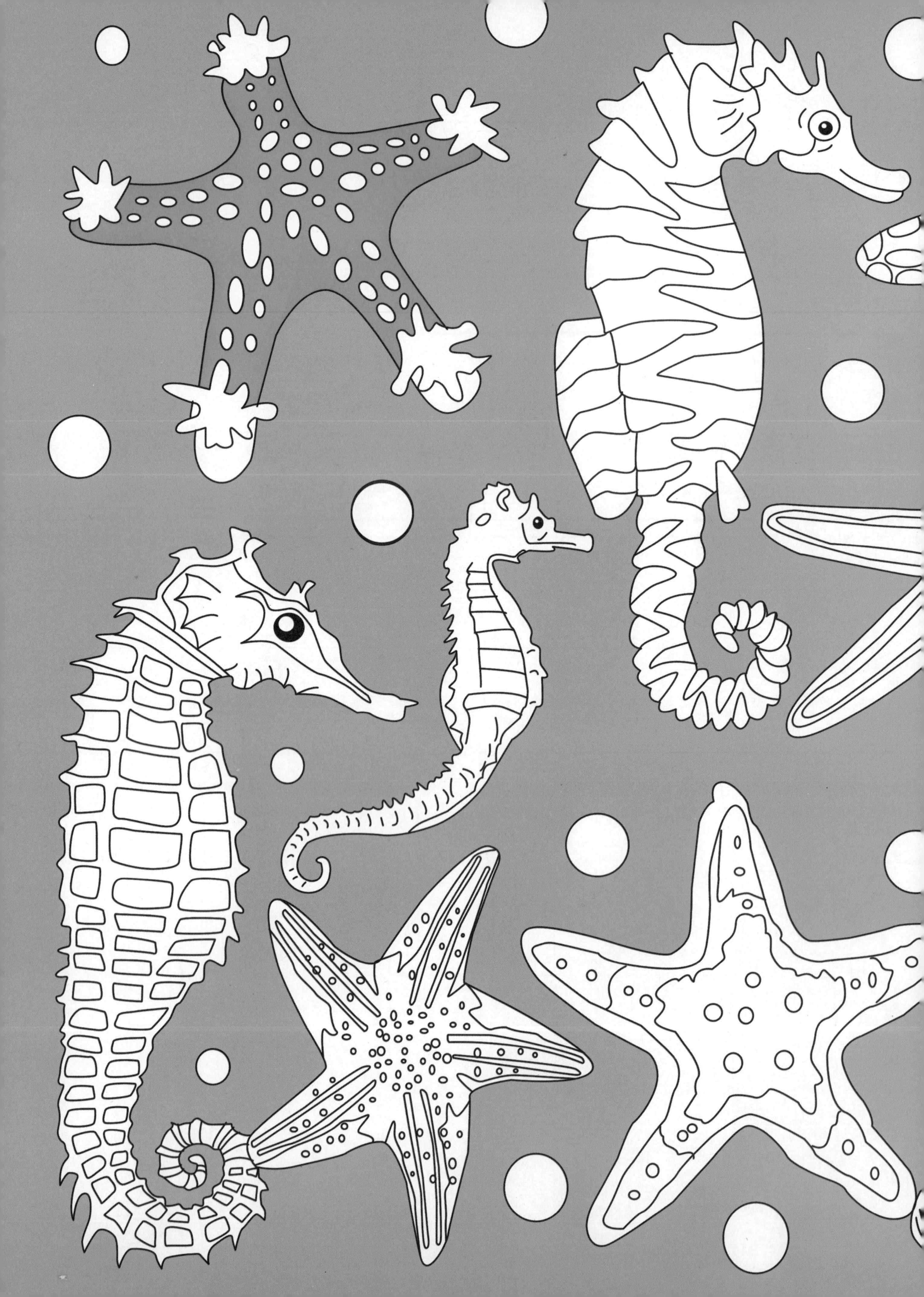

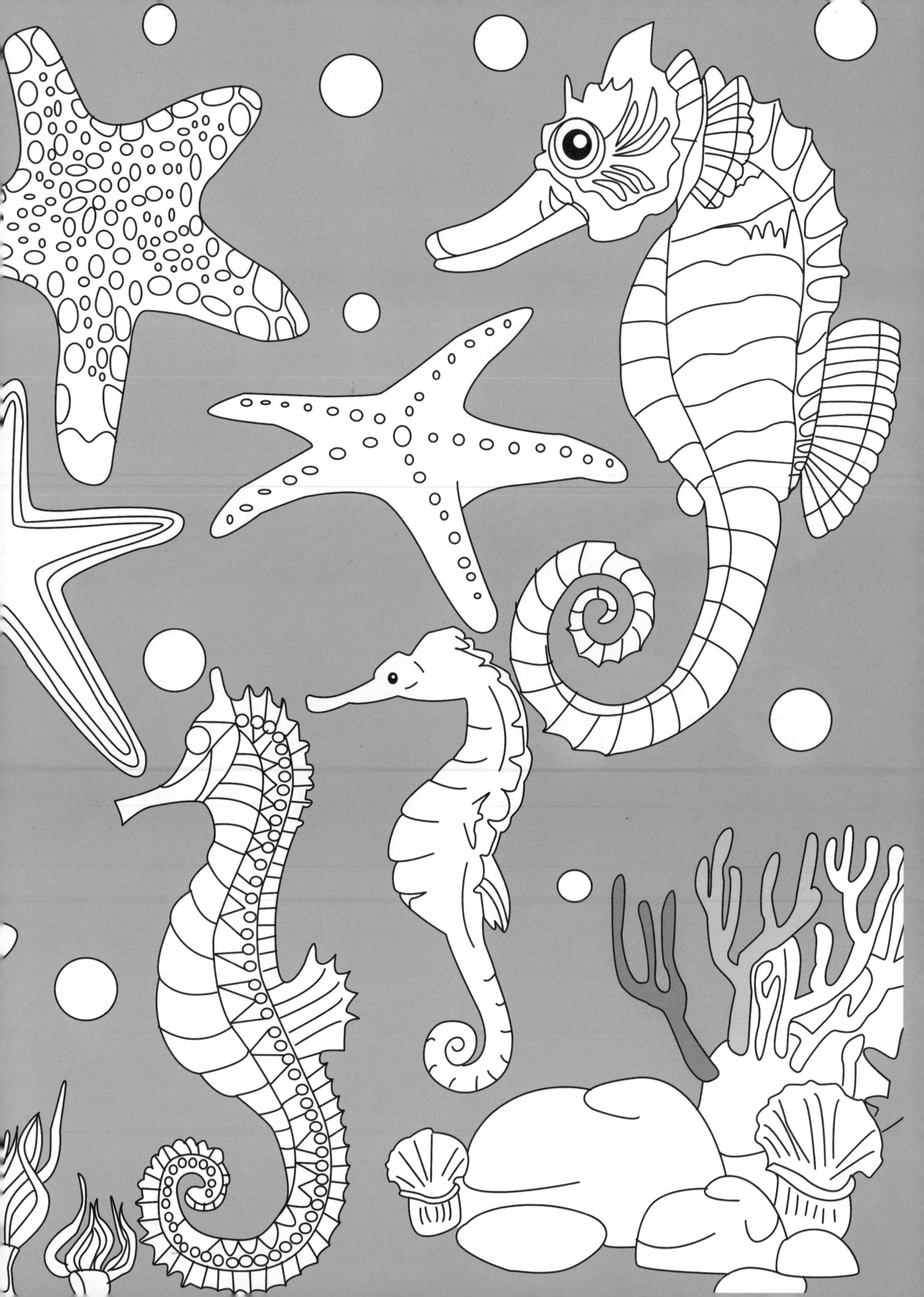